Contemporary SINGING Techniques

by Bob Rose

Disk in back of book – Please return to pocket when finished

ISBN 0-634-06721-4

HAL•LEONARD®
CORPORATION
7777 W. BLUEMOUND RD. P.O. BOX 13819 MILWAUKEE, WI 53213

In Australia Contact:
Hal Leonard Australia Pty. Ltd.
22 Taunton Drive P.O. Box 5130
Cheltenham East, 3192 Victoria, Australia
Email: ausadmin@halleonard.com

Visit Hal Leonard Online at
www.halleonard.com

CONTEMPORARY SINGING TECHNIQUES

by Bob Rose

ACKNOWLEDGMENTS

PRODUCTION, RECORDING AND EDITING: Bob Rose

AUDIO EDITING AND MASTERING: Joe Tarantino (Fantasy Records)

ART: COVER AND CD DESIGN AND BOOK LAYOUT: Linda Gough

BOOK ILLUSTRATIONS: Irene Taylor

TEXT EDITING AND CORRECTIONS: Darlene Anderson

WORD PROCESSING AND SETUP: Anthea Rose

This book is dedicated
to my wife, Anthea Rose,
for her ever-present faith,
patience and support
in this project.

Foreword

"...a musical approach to uncover and eliminate your technical problems..."

This audio program is designed to correct the most common singing and technical problems in addition to taking your voice into a new vocal ability, improving the technical and musical performance in your own desired style(s) when followed as instructed.

The following method contains a **male** or **female** CD with **Warm-Up Exercises, Segment 1** and **Singing Performance Sessions, Segment 2**. *Contemporary Singing Techniques* is designed to put in place the concept and experience of what your vocal instrument is and how to use it easily, both physically, and musically, with the least amount of resistance, while adding power, control and tonality at the same time.

This book is a **'Reference Text to an Audio CD'**. It's designed to be used as a reference and expansion to aid in visual clarity and additional information where time is a factor on the CD. It is not a book with CD examples. Used, as intended, *Contemporary Singing Techniques* will give you a musical approach to uncover and eliminate your technical problems.

<u>Important</u>

➤ **Remember that Segment 1 of the CD is set up with the instructor and piano on one side and the student and piano on the other. This way you can eliminate one side or the other if you wish to use the CD with 1) an accompaniment to emphasize more help or 2) your solo performance of an exercise for further development.**

CD Track Listing

WARM-UP EXERCISES (SEGMENT 1)

1. Introduction
2. Ex. #1 Chest/Lung Expansion
3. Ex. #2 Diaphragmatic Breathing
4. Ex. #3 The Yawn
5. Ex. #4 The Pant
6. Ex. #5 'Hey' Staccato
7. Ex. #6 'Hey' Sustained
8. Ex. #7 The Car Starting
9. Ex. #8 The Trill
10. Ex. #9 Humming
11. Ex. #10 Oral Placement
12. Ex. #11 Nasal Resonance & Release
13. Ex. #12 Throat Resonance
14. Ex. #13 Oral/Nasal/Throat Resonance
15. Ex. #14 Sob/Whine
16. Ex. #15 Good Vocal Posture
17. Conclusion

SINGING PERFORMANCE SESSIONS (SEGMENT 2)

18. Introduction
19. Instruction
20. Preliminary Vocal: Uncritiqued
21. I. Breath Support Session
22. II. Placement Session
23. III. Release – Resonance Session
24. Corrected Vocal Performance
25. The Song Trill
26. Music Track
27. Conclusion

Contents

Figure References Index

Introduction

"At each moment you choose the intentions that will shape your experiences and those things upon which you will focus your attention. If you choose unconsciously, you evolve unconsciously. If you choose consciously, you evolve consciously."

—Gary Zukav

Contemporary Singing Techniques is designed to **refocus your vocal efforts, eliminate the resistance** of your present approach, **freeing your voice** to sing from your diaphragm to your lips **without impedance.** This enables a **relaxed, open throat** and a **free-flowing air stream.** In fact, it ties your instrument's components and the mechanics of your whole voice together to work as one. *It's the mechanical link-up and its proper usage that assure an unobstructed operation of your instrument.*

The result is relaxation as well as a consistent and controlled air stream, enabling **increased power, range, pitch, endurance** and **ease of singing,** with connection, in any situation or style. To sing with connection is a matter of a **constant air stream adjustment,** note to note, from one end of your range to the other, leading to the development of a new sense-memory (i.e., experiencing a new feeling of what you need to do) note to note, vowel to vowel, extending and relaxing your whole range until it becomes second nature in your singing or speaking.

The following text is drawn mostly from the *Contemporary Singing Techniques* CD, with additional information for further clarification where the author felt it necessary.

CHAPTER I

Vocal Instrument Identification

The Voice as an Instrument

"...imagine....taking the mystery out of the process that has been holding you back in its operation."

As in using any other instrument, you must identify your vocal instrument and understand its components in addition to how they fit together and function.

These components unveil the mystery of the instrument's concealment, giving you a visual understanding as with any other instrument.

This enables you to imagine what's going on as you experience it, taking the mystery out of the process that has been holding you back in its operation.

Imagine playing an invisible piano, guitar, violin, saxophone, etc. It would be a great deal harder, wouldn't it?

INSTRUMENT COMPONENTS

(Refer to **Fig. 1A, 1B, 1C** for a visual of this chart)

The voice physiologically is composed of 4 parts:

1. <u>The Power Source</u> (the diaphragm/abdominal and intercostal muscles/lungs/trachea/bronchia)

2. <u>The Vibrators</u> (vocal cords/larynx)

3. <u>The Articulators</u> (teeth/lips/gum ridge/hard palate/soft palate/uvula)

4. <u>The Resonators</u> (nasal/oral/throat and occasional secondary resonators, chest and sinuses)

Singing/Speaking is composed of 4 components:

1. <u>Diaphragmatic Breathing</u> is accomplished a) by expanding the chest and b) letting air in and out through the stomach by lowering and raising the diaphragm. (*See* **Diaphragmatic Breathing, Pgs. 20-21.**)

2. <u>Breath Control</u> is the firming and the interaction of the abdominal and the diaphragm muscles to adjust the air stream to match the opening of the vocal cords. (*See* **The Abdominal Muscles, Pgs. 21-23**).

3. <u>Placement</u> is where the air stream and sound goes. (*See* **Oral and Nasal Placement, Pgs. 38-43.**)

4. <u>Release</u> is the **untrapping of the air stream** from impedances and resistance (on the way to the outside world).
   <u>a</u>) <u>Resonance</u> is the **expansion and reverberation** of the released sound in your resonant cavities, i.e., the nose, mouth, throat and occasionally the chest or sinuses. (*See* **Resonance, Pgs. 44-45.**)

Esthetic Characteristics:

1. <u>The Ear</u>: detection—application of aural (hearing) focus

2. <u>The Brain</u>: for establishing and retaining a sense-feel and sense-memory

3. <u>The Mind</u>: used in the awareness of your instrument, your music and the thought process

4. <u>The Emotions</u>: the connection and projection of your feelings; intent through interpretation

"You must know what the voice is made up of

and how it works to use it properly."

INSTRUMENT IDENTIFICATION

This figure is designed to point out the basic components of your instrument, providing an identification and reference.

Your voice is made up of many parts, not just the vocal cords. It is an instrument—in fact, a living instrument—and, therefore, must be identified, treated and used properly (as any instrument) for it to work unimpeded with its maximum potential.

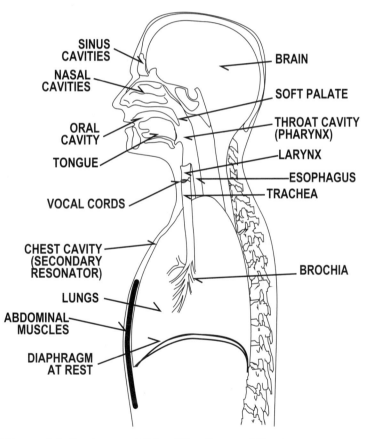

Figure 1A: Instrument Identification and Posture
Use this as a reference for the visualization of your instrument throughout this method.

Once the air stream is formed into pitch (via the vocal cords), it's brought up to the articulators and turned into specific sounds (e.g., vowels, consonants and words, etc.).

The articulators are composed of the **teeth, lips, gum ridge** (above the front teeth), the **hard palate** (the roof of the mouth), the **soft palate** (the flesh that hangs down from the top of the mid-mouth to the top of the throat), and the **uvula** (which dangles at the end of the soft palate and helps direct the air stream to the nose and the mouth). (*See* **Fig. 1B**.)

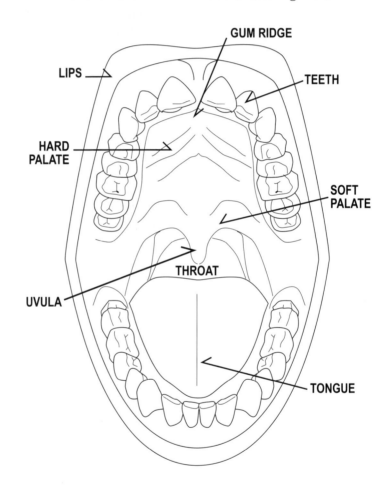

Figure 1B: Oral Articulators
Use this as a reference for the application of your articulators throughout this method.

The **larynx** is called the **voice box** because it contains the **vocal cords,** the **components** and the **cord muscles** that stretch and stabilize the vocal cords to adjust them to the air stream pressure coming from the diaphragm (the sub-glottal air stream). (*See* **Fig. 1A** for location and *see* **Glossary of Terms**).

The glottis is the space between the vocal cords (as represented in this figure by the dark area below). The vocal cords stretch (similar to a rubber band) to create higher pitches, making the air space smaller (i.e., closing) and more vertical between the vocal cords. In lower pitches, the glottis opens, making the air space larger (i.e., less vertical between the vocal cords).

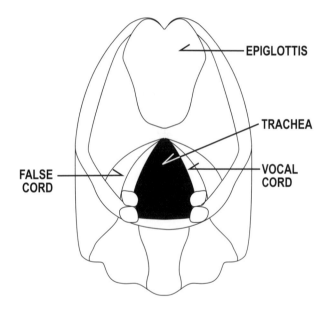

Figure 1C: The Larynx
Shown at rest (i.e., completely open).
Use this as a reference for the application of your vibrators throughout this method.

Note: *Try placing a rubber band between the thumb and the index finger, stretching and slacking to varying degrees, to see how the vocal cords elongate and contract for various pitches.*

CHAPTER 2

Vocal Hygiene

Vocal hygiene is the physical upkeep of your instrument, as it is living inside of you.

Just like the lubrication, tune-up and repair of your car, should you do any less for your instrument?

- In the first place, it's your body.

- Secondly, it's your instrument.

- Third, whether you sing for yourself, your friends or professionally, it's critical to keep an operational normality from day to day for your instrument or your health.

Allergy and Asthma Center of Austin

William C. Howland III, M.D.
Allergy and Immunology Specialist

August 14, 1997

To Whom It May Concern:

I have been receiving voice instruction from Bob Rose in Austin, Texas. I am
a physician specializing in allergy, immunology and asthma and I have been
particularly impressed with Mr. Rose's understanding of physiology and
respiratory anatomy. In fact, during my initial visits to his studio he explained
respiratory physiology and relationships to the function of the voice in
speaking and singing.

I found Mr. Rose's explanations to be both scientifically accurate and also
enlightening regarding the use of the voice. I feel that Mr. Rose is an excellent
voice teacher and personally have noted significant improvement in my singing
under his instruction. I am confident in recommending his skills to my patients
and also to professional colleagues and friends. I have also recommended
interaction between Mr. Rose and several of the ENT specialists in Austin
who deal with singers.

Sincerely,

William C. Howland III, M.D.

The voice is a **physical, mental** and **emotional** instrument. It is contained and living inside your body; therefore, all things that affect you, affect it—from your diet to your emotions. That is why it is important (and essential, in some cases) to follow a few simple health suggestions to help ensure your instrument's well-being. *Use the following list as a guideline only because all may not pertain to each individual and therefore must be considered prior to application, as well as consulting with your doctor or throat specialist (E.N.T./Laryngologist), if anything regarding your health or well-being is in question. The following are a few commonsense suggestions and are not intended to replace any doctor's advice or counsel nor claim to be a complete list for all vocal upkeep, but are generally satisfactory.*

Vocal Do's

- Check with your throat specialist prior to pursuing any vocal method or hygiene program if you experience an **irregularity** in your singing system or have any special considerations

- Get sufficient **sleep**

- Drink plenty of **water** (4-8 eight-ounce glasses per day, build up slowly)

- Drink **herbal tea** for opening up, warming and soothing the throat and nasals, but follow with water, as tea may have a tendency to dry you out prior to singing

- **Gargle** morning and evening (more frequently, if needed) with a light, to-the-taste **salt-water solution** (a 1/4 teaspoon in a cup of lukewarm water). You may also add a pinch of baking soda to the water, if you desire. Also, occasionally gargle with plain cold tap water (i.e., nothing added) to help cool down an irritated throat

- **Steam your lungs and vocal cords** by taking deep breaths in the shower

- **Steam** whenever the nasals or throat are clogged up from sinus congestion, a cold, smog, smoke, etc. Use a **personal steamer** or simply **boil a pan of water**, place it on a counter or table and inhale the vapor with a towel over your head like a tent (making sure that you do not get too close to the pan, which could cause a serious burn). **When mucus is loosened, gargle it out.**

- To open clogged **nasals**: Use (a) a saline solution nasal spray and (b) an opening nose strip or (c) spread sides of nose apart with thumbs and index finger (by pushing outward on the sides) for a quick opening only

- **Suck on** natural (i.e., chemical-free) **throat lozenges** (sugar-free, if possible) as needed, unless the throat is inflamed, then

- **Suck on slippery elm throat lozenges** for an irritated or sore throat or crush and add to tea

- **Use an antacid** when needed to avoid heartburn or acid reflux, which causes repetitive burning of throat tissues and vocal cords (check with your pharmacist or doctor)

- **Buy a saline solution spray** (i.e., light, purified salt water) and spray the nasal passages and the throat daily as many times as needed to loosen mucus and soothe irritated tissue (there are no active chemicals in most saline solutions as there are in a decongestant spray)

- **Treat cold sores** in your mouth with a liquid or a gel product specifically for cold sores

- **Use petroleum jelly** on the edge of your irritated nasals or on chapped lips (if needed)

- **Use a mucus thinner/decongestant cough suppressant** when needed (consult with your doctor or pharmacist)

Vocal Don'ts

- **Avoid** dairy products. They tend to produce mucus in your throat as they are ingested, and, when metabolized as well. *Talk to your doctor regarding any bodily nutrition you may be deriving from dairy products.*

- **Limit coffee** intake. Use decaffeinated whenever possible, (caffeine is a diuretic and dries you out). Try to avoid coffee completely before or during a performance (counteract caffeine consumption by drinking a lot of water).

- **Don't consume** lemon or any **citrus** before performing as they contain **acids**, which irritate your throat. Also try cutting down as a general rule (they produce mucus).

- **Don't consume vinegar, hard alcohol** or **spicy food** when your throat is irritated or before performing. In general, it is also advisable to cut down on these as well.

- **Avoid milk chocolate**, especially prior to performances or singing (as it produces mucus).

- **Avoid** peanuts, popcorn, crackers, or other **dry foods** before performing, as they absorb water from your system, dry out your throat and stick to your mouth, throat, and articulators.

- **Avoid** gargling with mouthwashes or medicated sprays (they can dry or burn the throat and cause mucus). Check with a throat specialist (E.N.T.) and/or a pharmacist if you need medical attention for the best medication for your health and voice. Mouthwash is fine when used in the mouth only (do not gargle with it).

- **Don't consume sugar or sweets** before a performance, as they produce mucus.

- **Do not smoke** or inhale smoke. First- or second-hand smoke is an irritant and a health hazard, as confirmed by the Surgeon General, and it causes mucus as well as the possibility of an uncontrolled, raspy voice.

- **Don't eat within two to four hours**, depending on the size of the meal (the smaller the better), before performing due to the interaction between the diaphragm and the digestive system (also, to avoid acid reflux, heartburn or other stomach reactions).

- **Avoid decongestants,** which dry you out. **Use only those that thin, not harden mucus** when necessary. A good mucus-thinner is appropriate. Check with your doctor or pharmacist.

- **Don't neglect your medical care,** which may allow a condition to continue without your awareness (consult with a qualified E.N.T.)

VOCALLY ABUSIVE BEHAVIORS

These suggestions are main topics, not a complete list. They will, however, provide you with the basis for better vocal behaviors.

<u>Vocal Don'ts</u>

- **Incorrect vocal posture**—instrument being shaped incorrectly, causing poor performance

- **Inadequate sleep,** causing fatigue or laziness in the voice

- **Overuse or fatigue** of your vocal instrument: **singing or speaking**

- **Lack of a good vocal technique** (reverting to poor, injurious habits)

- **Public speaking or singing** without correct breath support and control

- Emotional performances **without technical control**

- Singing, speaking **too loudly**

- **Shouting** or screaming

- Hard/Continuous talking

- **Clearing** your throat constantly (it causes irritation and indicates a physical or habitual problem)

- **Using your voice** while it is irritated or injured, especially with laryngitis (an irritation of the vocal cords)

- Unaddressed **negative dietary or allergic effects**
  a) use of **mucus-producing** products
  b) induced **irritations** (diet, heartburn, etc.)
  c) **dehydration** (not drinking enough water and/or drinking diuretics)
  d) **neglected allergies** not properly treated (i.e., for a singer)

- Using **medications** that dry you out (check with your doctor or pharmacist)

- Not addressing a **chronic medical problem** (consult with an E.N.T.)

- **Inhaling smoke,** whether first-hand or second-hand

- **Prolonged inhaling of chemicals,** occasionally or consistently, (causing throat and lung irritation)

- Not taking **preventive or curative measures** for any vocal or health abnormalities

THE VOCALIST'S GIG BAG

Keep the following in a good toiletry bag with as many compartments as possible. Use containers to keep contents fresh and refill or change regularly. Don't get sloppy. Keep a fresh supply, as you never know when you'll need something for good vocal hygiene at any time. Also, keep all containers and items clean or discarded when not sanitary. This list is only the basics for normal upkeep and not intended to be complete for each individual. Add any of your own specific needs.

Contemporary Singing Techniques

Item	Amount	Description	Purpose
1	1 Container	Fresh, natural spring water	Keep throat lubricated and body hydrated
2	1 Container	Watertight (with 3 oz. of salt)	For light salt-water gargle to remove mucus (*see* **Vocal Hygiene**)
3	1	Collapsible (or small travel) cup	For gargling with salt-water
4	1 Container	Saline nasal/throat spray (non-medicated)	To clear nasals/vocal cords and throat
5	2	Medicinal brand 'Breathe Easy' herbal tea bags	To soothe throat
6	1 Pkg.	Non-medicated natural throat lozenges (sugar-free if possible)	To soothe minor sore throat or just for lubrication
7	1 Pkg.	Slippery elm throat lozenges	For soothing irritated throat
8	1 Container	Mucus thinner/decongestant cough suppressant only when needed (consult your doctor or pharmacist)	To thin mucus when needed for colds, allergies, etc. to keep from drying out and coughing to a minimal
9	4	Nasal strips (nasal openers)	For stuffy nose, sinuses, etc.
10	1 Container	Antacid tablets	For acid reflux or heartburn (as directed by doctor or pharmacist)
11	1 Small container	Petroleum Jelly	To lubricate irritated nose, mouth, lips
12	1 Small tube	Cold sore gel	For cold sores or irritations
13	6	Cotton-tipped applicators	To apply Petroleum Jelly or gel
14	1 Vial	High-quality allergenic eyedrops	For smoke, lubrication, sinuses
15	1	Toothbrush/Toothpaste	To brush teeth and tongue

Important

1) *Listen* to the CD (**Segments 1 and 2**) at least one time through, referring to this text as a guide, and then as a reference when needed.

2) **Refer to each figure** in this text as indicated on CD (**warm-ups and sessions**) for a general visual understanding.

3) **Begin vocalizing** with the complete vocal **warm-up, Segment 1** and continue using it on a regular basis for vocal development (after a while you may want to use the short version, number 5 of this page).

4) **Use the scales** in every exercise, but this time **with your balance control** turned all the way in one direction (left or right)
   a) to omit the student track to give you just a music track to practice with or
   b) in the other direction for more support from the student track

5) For warm-up prior to singing, **use a short version of the warm-up** segment for daily practice, using **Exercises 1, 2, 3, 7, 8, 9, 10, 13 and 15**.

6) **Follow along with the singing-performance, Segment 2** to familiarize yourself with the method.

7) **Use the performance, Segment 2** for practice and concept for your own material.

8) **Use the music tracks in Segment 2** to record your performance until you're ready to use the method on your own material.

9) **Apply the sessions (Segment 2) to your own repertoire**, using the **Session Aids** for practice purposes on your own lyric sheets, making notes as a road map to improve your performance as the example lyric sheet in the session's song.

CHAPTER 3

Male and Female Warm-up Exercises

(CD Segment 1)

Grammy in the Schools
Presented by *The Recording Academy* at the
University of Texas, Austin 1997

Classes and Seminars
At the acclaimed *Learning Tree University*
in Los Angeles, California 1991

Introduction

For all of the figure references on the CD, see the illustrations in this text.

Note: *Exercises 1- 6 can be done **just about anywhere,** while Exercises 7-15 require **more focus** and **concentration,** and therefore, should be confined to a more suitable atmosphere.*

*Finally, the correct use of this CD will produce excellent results. You must pay **close attention** to the exercises and text to **execute the method correctly.** Always make sure you begin in good physical voice.*

Important Note: *If you feel there are any problems with your voice prior to embarking on any vocal program, check with a vocal specialist such as an E.N.T. or laryngologist.*

Concept

The following exercises are:

1) **Narrated**

2) **Instructed and**

3) **Demonstrated** by students while the instructor critiques them to uncover typical problems the student is having that often occur with many vocalists.

Segment 1 is provided to:

1) **Warm up**

2) **Open**

3) **Stretch**

4) **Align and**

5) **Direct your voice toward its optimum performance**

"Chest expansion keeps the upper portion of the lungs open and expanded...creating a good vocal posture and encouraging the diaphragm and lower lungs to do their job in deep breathing."

Exercise #1 ▶ <u>Chest/Lung Expansion</u>

Concept

Chest expansion keeps the upper portions of the lungs open and expanded via the intercostal (i.e., rib) muscles (*see* **Fig. 2B**). Therefore, enlisting the aid of the atmospheric pressure @ 15 lbs. per square inch, helping to open up the lungs, creating the basis of a good vocal posture and encouraging the diaphragm and lower lungs to do their job in deep breathing (*see* **Fig. 3**). This is what the expansion of the chest is setting them up to do unlike the state of a normal respiratory system, which is basically in a semi-collapsed state most of the time (*see* **Fig. 2A**).

Application

Standing sideways to a mirror:

1) Take a deep breath, expanding the chest (rib) muscles, while creating a good internal posture

2) Hold the chest in place via the intercostal muscles (*see* **Fig. 2B**)

3) Breathe in and out through the stomach while watching in the mirror to see that only the stomach is moving while the chest remains stable in its expanded position encouraging deep (or stomach) breathing in and out (*see* **Figs. 2D, 4A and 4B**)

Collapsed/Expanded Chest

The following figures show the chest from normal to expanded. Expanding the chest cavity establishes a good posture from the inside out, opening up and staying open—instead of tightening up the back muscles, which creates tension and strain.

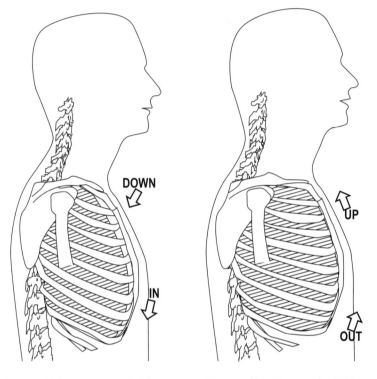

Figure 2A: Collapsed Chest
(Poor Posture)
The chest in a normal position.

Figure 2B: Expanded Chest
(Good Posture) The chest open and responding to the atmospheric pressure.

Collapsed/Expanded Lungs

When the chest is expanded, it keeps the lungs open (*see* **Fig. 2D**). This is what I refer to as a Good Vocal Posture for maximum vocal efficiency.

The following figures show the lungs from collapsed (i.e., their normal state, *see* **Fig. 2C**) to expanded (as in singing, *see* **Fig. 2D**). Taking a <u>deep</u> breath expands the lungs. The lungs stay expanded by keeping the chest expanded as previously explained.

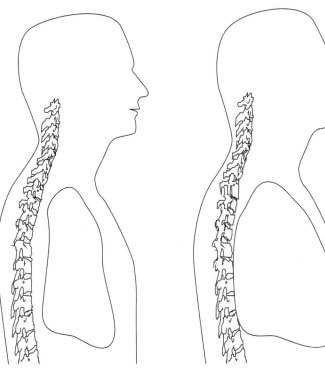

Figure 2C: Collapsed Lungs— Encouraging a poor vocal posture and leaving the lungs drained of air.

Figure 2D: Expanded Lungs— Encouraging a good vocal posture and keeping the upper lungs filled with air.

"Your instrument is like an automobile. Air is your fuel, the diaphragm is like the accelerator, and you must have a full tank to perform and sustain a note to its maximum capacity. If not, you're only running on fumes."

Exercise #2 ▶ **Diaphragmatic Breathing**

Concept

Your instrument is like an automobile. Air is your fuel, the diaphragm is like the accelerator, and your lungs are your tank to sustain a note to its maximum capacity. If not, you're only running on fumes (i.e., not enough air).

When breathing from the diaphragm, which is the large muscle at the bottom of the lungs (*see* **Fig. 3**), **you inhale**, causing it to move downward and expand, pushing your stomach out. **When you exhale**, it contracts, moving upward causing your stomach to move in. This is called **diaphragmatic** or **stomach breathing**.

Application

Practice Diaphragmatic (or stomach) **Breathing** (*see* **Fig. 4A and 4B**), keeping the expanded chest posture to initiate lower-lung breathing.
A. **Inhale**: the stomach expands, moving out (*see* **Fig. 4A**).
B. **Exhale**: the stomach contracts, moving in (*see* **Fig. 4B**), while the chest remains in its expanded position.

Additional Applications

• *Monitor the motion by putting your hand on your stomach to feel the motion of deep breathing while keeping your chest in its expanded position (see* **Fig. 2B**).

• *Watch this in a mirror until you're experiencing it happening automatically (i.e., a sense-feel to a sense-memory, see* **Glossary of Terms**).

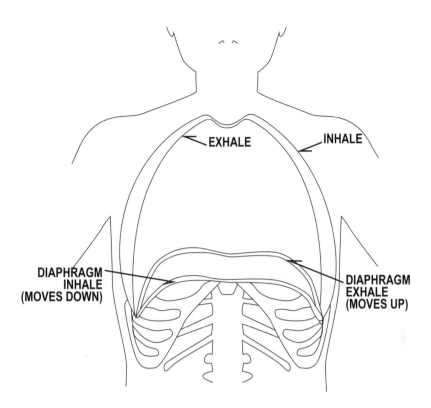

Figure 3: Diaphragmatic Motion
This figure illustrates where the diaphragm and chest travel begins and ends. The arrows show the direction it is moving when inhaling and exhaling.

THE ABDOMINAL MUSCLES

(Reference to Exercises 2, 4, 5, 6, & 7)

When exhaling, with the abdominal (stomach) muscle firmed, the diaphragm will become firm as well; therefore, it will control the speed of the air for singing and speaking just as a car accelerator controls the flow of gas (and so the speed) of the car. You will experience this in **Exercise #6**, the 'Sustained Hey'.

"The key to an effective and relaxed voice is to balance the air pressure, using enough to excite pitch and tone without using too much, which pushes the larynx into the upper throat (breathing passage), causing a break in the air stream and/or pulling the vocal cords apart as well."

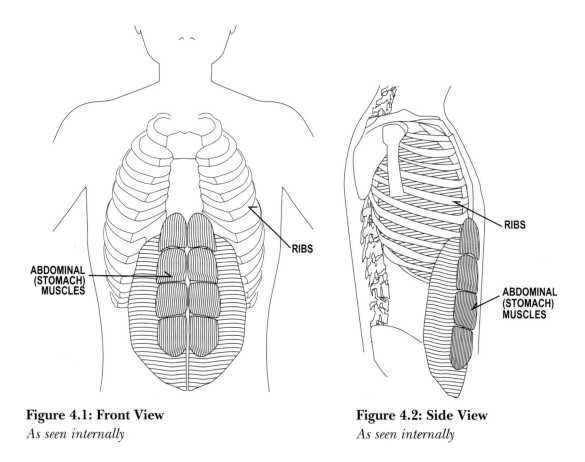

Figure 4.1: Front View
As seen internally

Figure 4.2: Side View
As seen internally

This shows the muscles of the abdomen (stomach) from both positions. The muscles firm to create control with the interaction of the diaphragm.

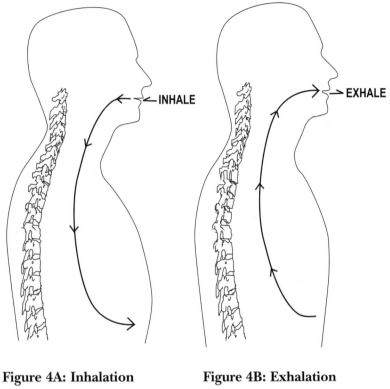

Figure 4A: Inhalation
The stomach moves out.

Figure 4B: Exhalation
The stomach moves in.

After your chest is expanded and you're breathing from the diaphragm, air will expand and contract your lower lungs. Watch yourself in a mirror to observe your stomach as you do **Exercises 2, 4, 5, 6, and 7**.

The Yawn
(Full-Partial)

Concept

A full yawn (as you would do naturally) is used for stretching and relaxing facial and neck muscles. Yawning **opens, stretches and releases** the face and throat muscles. Like a runner stretching before running, a singer, too, must stretch before singing (*see* **Fig. 5C**). (For facial relaxation relating to a yawn, *see* **Fig. 12: Facial, Jaw and Chin Muscles.**)

A partial yawn will drop the larynx down, opening up the throat for release and depth of resonance in exercises and singing (*see* **Fig. 5D**). Also, activating these throat muscles, stabilizing the larynx, keep it from moving up into the breathing passage in the upper throat when singing higher notes.

Note: *Most of the following exercises and singing will include a partial to a half-yawn, keeping the larynx from moving up into the breathing passage.*

Application

1) **Yawn fully**, several times, feeling the sensation and the full dropping of the larynx. Feel the stretch and the muscle release. This is the best relaxation for the face and throat.

2) **Yawn partially** while speaking like a low-sounding cartoon character, releasing the yawn from time to time to hear and feel the difference. Your voice seems to shift although it's just the throat opening up then returning to normal like the way your voice sounds when you first wake up from sleeping and you're yawning as you speak.

These examples show a comparison between the larynx at rest (**Fig. 5A**) and the various other positions (**Figs. 5B, 5C, and 5D**).

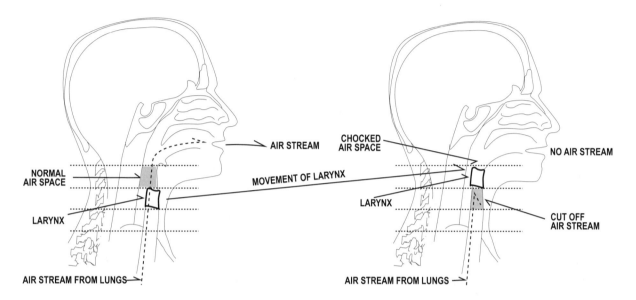

Figure 5A: The Larynx at Rest
The larynx at rest represents a normal state of relaxation. However, for singing, this state must be aided by activating the same muscles used in a yawn to stabilize the larynx and keep it from traveling upward as the notes get higher, as well as adding low resonance.

Figure 5B: The Larynx Raised
On the other hand, a raised larynx that goes too high in the throat will cut off the breathing passage, causing breaks in the air stream and, therefore, the sound, as well as causing compression in the throat (i.e., pushing the larynx up) and at times pulling the vocal cords apart.

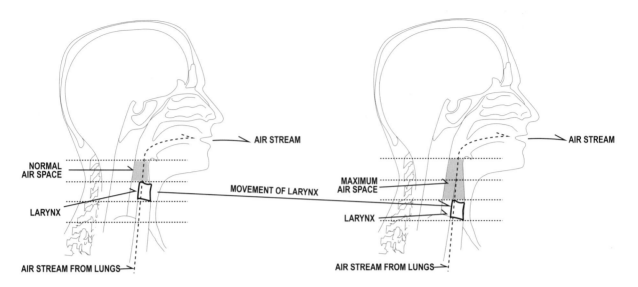

Figure 5A: The Larynx at Rest
The larynx at rest represents a normal state of relaxation. However, for singing, this state must be aided by activating the same muscles used in a yawn to stabilize the larynx and keep it from traveling upward as the notes get higher, as well as adding low resonance.

Figure 5C: The Larynx Dropped
Dropping the larynx, as in a complete yawn, releases the throat and facial muscles by stretching as you open and relaxing as you release.

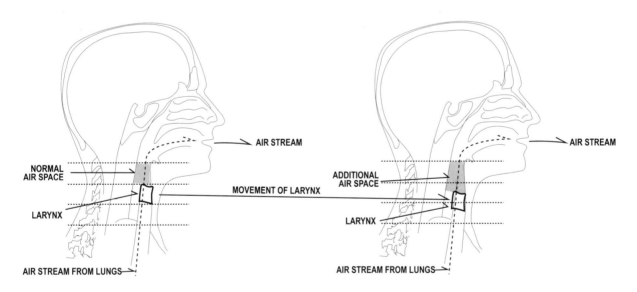

Figure 5A: The Larynx at Rest
The larynx at rest represents a normal state of relaxation. However, for singing, this state must be aided by activating the same muscles used in yawn to stabilize the larynx and keep it from a traveling upward as the notes get higher, as well as adding low resonance.

Figure 5D: The Larynx Partially Dropped
A partially dropped larynx is accomplished by a partial yawn, bringing the larynx down away from the breathing passage for singing, as well as opening up the throat for additional low-end resonance. Try using a low-sounding cartoon character.
(*Listen* to the CD.)

Exercise #4 ▶ <u>The Pant</u>

Concept

In a pant (like a dog), the stomach moves quickly, going in as you exhale and almost falling out as you almost automatically inhale. Because your chest is expanded, you set yourself up to breathe naturally through the lower lungs (stomach). Panting is the beginning of becoming aware of and building up both your stomach and your diaphragm muscles and the interaction between them, leading to greater breath control and easier, more powerful singing. I call this a *vocal sit-up*.

Application

1) Now, let's **pant** like a dog. Notice that with the chest in place (*see* **Fig. 2B**), after you exhale, (*see* **Fig. 4B**) the air rushes back into the lower lungs automatically (*see* **Fig. 4A**) practically inhaling for you because you are set up for this to happen by the chest expansion (*see* **Fig. 2B** and *listen* to the CD).

Additional Applications

- *Add a **partial yawn** (see **Fig.5D**) to experience more air flowing through the throat with a little deeper tone because it lowers the larynx, creating a little larger cavity.*

- *Remember to **monitor** with your hand on your stomach, to become aware of and experience the pulse and motion. (Stand sideways to a mirror, observing this experience.)*

'Hey' Staccato

Concept/Application

I call this **'Hey' Staccato.** Saying 'hey,' contracts the stomach in a rapid motion, causing a firmness in the stomach. This is a natural response. To add stability to the larynx, use a partial yawn at the same time, saying the 'hey' in your mouth while engaging the abdominal and diaphragmic muscles to initiate and control the sparse air stream spurts. (*Listen* to the CD.)

This not only eliminates a lot of fatigue in the throat, but also initiates the air from the bottom of the lungs (i.e., bringing air up from below). Adding a little diaphragmatic punch and a partial yawn sends the air stream to the mouth and nasals **through** the throat (not with it or in it), eliminating possible discomfort or damage to your voice from a choked airflow (*see* **Fig. 4A and 4B** for stomach motion).

Additional Applications

- *Add a **partial yawn** for openness of the throat.*

Concept

This is like the 'Hey' Staccato, but holding the note out as you would in singing, keeping the stomach firm for a longer period of time to **sustain the sound comfortably to a close** (i.e., stop). This is accomplished by sustaining the interaction between the abdominal and diaphragm muscles, creating a controlled resistance that regulates the air stream to be used and keeps the diaphragm firmed to controlling its rate of speed and, therefore, the air stream (as the accelerator). **This is how the breath is controlled for singing**. Feel the **sustained firmness** in your stomach as you are exhaling, experiencing the air moving out at a consistent rate rather than randomly. **Take in a breath while releasing the muscles instantaneously** so that you take in air quickly, **always through the mouth. When inhaling, feel the expansion of your diaphragm and stomach.**

Application

For the first three notes, do as 'Hey' Staccato (**Exercise 6**), then on the fourth note, firm the stomach and exhale to release the air evenly, steadily, and slowly with a controlled air stream for singing or exercising (*see* **Fig. 4A** and **4B** for stomach motion and *listen* to the CD).

This is the key **to good entrances, exits, phrasing, and pitch,** as well as **holding and closing notes and words.**

Additional Applications

- *Monitor your support as before, viewing the exercise in a mirror at first.*
- *Begin with the **'hey' sustained**, forgoing the first three 'hey' staccatos.*
- *Add a **partial yawn** for openness of the throat.*

▶ <u>**The Car Starting**</u>

Concept

The sound of an old car trying to start (i.e., cranking) but not actually starting. This is like a pant with a sustained pulse of sound and is also the basis of a **diaphragmatic vibrato**, as well as being the best vocal sit-up I know. Once you are comfortable with this exercise, you may substitute it for **Exercises 5 and 6** of your daily routine. (*See* **Fig. 4A and 4B** for abdominal motion and *listen* to the CD.)

Application

Begin with:

1. *A cappella* (without music or scales)

Then go to:

2. Scales (adding a partial yawn)

Additional Applications

- *Always go back to the pant if you're having any problems with this exercise. Then return to this exercise.*

- *Keep the pulse regular and even. If necessary, slow it down until this is accomplished. Then return to normal speed.*

- *Add a **partial yawn** for openness of the throat.*

"For many reasons, trilling is a good monitor for exercises or singing as there are no words, vowel sounds, or consonants to interrupt the flow of air or take the ear's attention away from the operation of your instrument."

Exercise #8 ➤ <u>The Trill</u>

Concept

Trilling the tongue or the lips by:

1. Using the **tongue** (*see* **Fig. 6**) or

2. Using the **lips** (*see* **Fig. 7**)

It's your choice. Either one will work. I call this an **infinite consonant**, which is stopping the air flow on and off using a constant air stream. For many reasons, trilling is a good monitor for exercises or singing as there are no words, vowel sounds, or consonants to interrupt the flow of air stream or take the ear's attention away from the operation of your instrument. Your whole singing system is now given the ability to operate with **an unimpeded, controlled air stream** while giving you the opportunity of just **hearing what you're singing**: the pitch, the placement, the resonance and air flow without interruption, just a constant pulse that you will even out as you practice it. (*Listen* to the CD).

Quick Check

Remember to **1) maintain a firm stomach** as you exhale so that your air is **completely controlled** (by your diaphragm) while you **2) use a partial yawn** to keep your larynx down and **3) release some air through the nasals** during trilling (like a silent hum). Remember to **4) relax your chin and facial muscles** without any contortions (monitor in a mirror). These four basics allow the air to flow continuously through your throat, mouth and nasals. (*See* **Figs. 6, 7, and 8**.)

"The better you can trill a song, the better you will sing it."

THE TONGUE TRILL

Instruction/Application

1) Position your tongue toward the front of the hard palate just behind the gum ridge above the top teeth (not on them) where the tongue feels relaxed.

2) To get started, you may want to use little percussive blasts of air from the diaphragm until you can sustain the trill.

3) Use an 'R' sound to aid the tongue in its proper positioning off the sides of the teeth keeping it from sticking if necessary. (*See* **Fig. 6** and *listen* to the CD.)

This may take a little time so be patient, *listen* **to the CD and practice, practice, practice!**

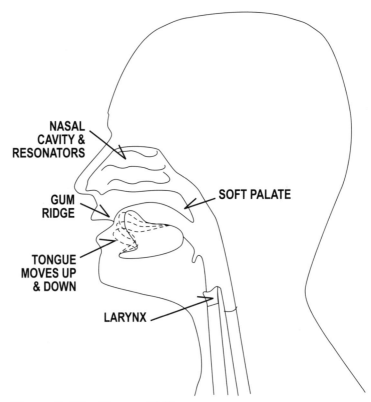

NASAL
CAVITY &
RESONATORS

SOFT PALATE

GUM
RIDGE

TONGUE
MOVES UP
& DOWN

LARYNX

Figure 6: The Tongue Trill

Instruction

Trill with your lips by simply 1) making a sound like a horse, relaxing the lips and 2) initiating it with a glottal attack (*see* **Glossary of Terms**) to get the feel and a start. 3) *Listen* to **Exercise 6**, but use your lips (*see* **Fig. 7**). With a good air stream and relaxed lips, try 4) sustaining the sound as you hear it on the CD, but using the lips.

Application
(Tongue and Lip)

Using a tongue or lip trill apply:
1) A siren sound from your low- to high-range
2) A scale
a) Add a partial yawn to lower your larynx
b) Add a partial hum to open a nasal release and resonance
c) Combine the yawn and hum together with these exercises for release and resonance

(*See* **Fig. 6 and 7** and *listen* to the CD).

This may take a little time, so be patient, **listen to the CD and practice, practice, practice.**

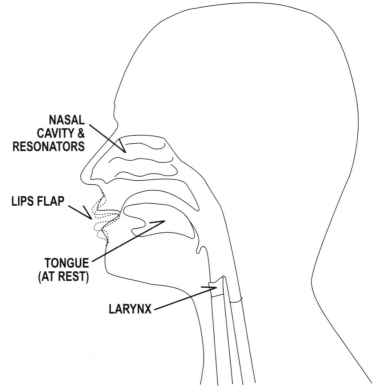

NASAL CAVITY & RESONATORS

LIPS FLAP

TONGUE (AT REST)

LARYNX

Figure 7: The Lip Trill

Additional Applications

- *When you feel you are doing the exercise well, trill a song melody all the way through. The better you can trill a song, the better you will sing it. Also, it will help you to warm up to that particular song. Try it and feel the difference!* (*Listen* to the example in **Segment 2**, Track 25 of the CD.)

"Humming opens and releases the nasals."

Exercise #9 ▶ **Humming**

Concept

Humming opens your nasal cavities, giving you a release for the air stream as it works its way **through your throat into the nose** and out into the world. It's also nice for opening up your nasal cavities for resonance, as well.

Add a little hum to exercises or singing and notice the release in your throat in addition to an increase in resonance. Hums can be silent for the sake of release or they can be aural for the sake of resonance and style. You choose. It's the difference between letting a little air move through or amplifying the sound into the nose as well. (This will be covered in more depth in **Exercise 11, Nasal Resonance and Release**).

Make sure the sound goes only to the nasals on high notes, no matter how small it feels, as you are only concerned with placement in the nose and release from the throat at this time (*see* **Fig 8**). As the exercise becomes more comfortable, open up and direct a little more air into the nose, mouth and throat by means of a partial yawn (without dropping the note back). This will broaden the resonance, make the highs fuller, even out, and adjust the tone to your taste (*see* **Fig. 8**).

Instruction/Application

To open the nasal cavity for release and/or resonance, hum the following exercises:

1) *A cappella*

Then:

2) Scales using
   a) 'M' - Mid-back nasal resonance (occurring in the back of the nose for a fuller sound)
   b) 'N' - Front nasal resonance (occurring in front of the nose for a brighter sound)
   c) 'M' to 'N' to 'M', etc. (to experience the release, feeling, placement and sound differences)
   (*See* **Fig. 8** and *listen* to the CD).

Additional Applications

* *Imagine the air stream getting smaller as the notes rise in pitch and travel toward the nose.*

* *Imagine the note shrinking and moving upward to the nasals.*

* *Add a partial yawn, when you're ready, to keep the larynx from moving up, which helps the flow of air, as well as adding some low resonance.*

* *Add a little glottal attack (see **Glossary of Terms**) directed toward the nose to help direct the air stream upward.*

* *Speak and sing into the nose (an exaggeration) to get the <u>feel</u> until it is natural to include the nasals regularly in your execution of sound, like a ventriloquist.*

* *Apply the 'M' and 'N' release silently to all exercises and songs to the degree of sound (tonality) you desire to create.*

Advanced

* *Give a little whine like a puppy into your nose for high notes, as this will help establish the air stream and expand the sound in the nasals as well as stabilize the vocal cords (after experiencing **Exercise 14**).*

Release/Resonance

The nasal cavities provide two basic functions:

1) **a release** for supra-glottal (above the vocal cords) air pressure, and

2) **a resonator** for mid-range articulation and fullness

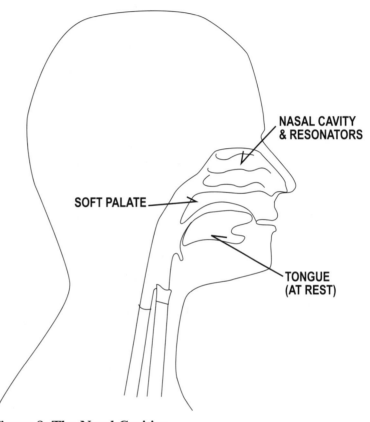

Figure 8: The Nasal Cavities
As the pitch rises, the sound waves become smaller and travel in the direction of smaller cavities such as the nose.

"To sing with good placement is a matter of a constant air stream adjustment, note to note, from one end of your range to the other."

Exercise #10 ▶ <u>Oral Placement</u>
<u>Articulator/Amplifier/Resonator</u>

Concept

The oral cavity makes up the final area in which the sound is converted into intelligible words as well as being amplified. It may also be resonated along with the nasal and throat cavities. Here the pitch, volume and color are turned into intelligible sounds in various proportions, depending on the user's ability.

The oral cavity (i.e., the mouth) provides your instrument with four basic functions:

1) **Articulation**, which brings enunciation to the sound (i.e., completed sounds, consonants, words, etc.) (*See* **Fig. 1B**)

2) **Amplification**, which adds volume to the sound by opening up the mouth and directing more air into it.

3) **Resonance**, which adds tonal quality to the sound, and

4) **Release** to the throat, opening it to let the air stream flow forward more easily.

Note: *You will not only come to experience a sense-feel but develop a sense-memory for the operation of this component. Also, you will learn how to use it individually or in various combinations with the nose and throat. (Listen to the CD regarding resonance.)*

Oral placement is basically bringing sounds forward into the mouth. Especially moving the sounds that fall back into the throat (choking off the air stream) and redirecting them into the mouth. **This does not mean pulling them from the throat up to the mouth**, as that creates a resistance and compression in the throat many singers experience on mid-range to higher notes as the larynx rises. (*See* **Fig. 5A and 5B.**)

Rather, it is a focusing forward using a frontal voice, establishing the feeling of sound generating from the front of the mouth (as in your speaking). This will feel somewhat exaggerated, at first, but will help you to gain a sense-feel of where the sound should be. The sound is at ease and most effective when you feel the forward placement. Gradually you will add throat and nasal resonance for more tonal depth (by means of a partial yawn and a hum) once you feel comfortable keeping your note in place, (i.e., forward) out of the throat after establishing a sense memory.

By modifying the sound, you are clearing up and directing it so as not to resist the air stream, which carries it. Each note must be adjusted over your whole range to maintain a relatively even air stream throughout a song or exercise without causing pressure in your throat. The pressure will make you lose connection from either straining or going to falsetto (a breathy false-cord release)—both of which are poor alternatives to a **well-placed full voice.**

Preliminary Application

The following modifications use the most common sounds, but this concept may be applied to any sounds you may have trouble with. (*See* **Sound Modifications Chart.**)

Say 'E' (which occurs in the front of the mouth) and then say 'A' (which normally begins in the back of the mouth); then with the 'E' placement (which is in the front of the mouth). Say 'E', 'A', 'E', 'A' in the same place in your mouth (i.e., the front 'E' placement). As an aid, use a little cartoon character sound that is placed very forward in the mouth to hold the placement.

The first vowel sets up the placement of the second vowel. The second vowel 'A' (being the back vowel) is brought forward into the mouth by the forward vowel 'E', leading the 'A' to be pronounced in the same spot as the 'E' and keeping the back vowel from interrupting or impeding the air stream. Then, closing with the 'E', keeps it all forward from beginning to the end. (*See* **Fig. 9** and *listen* to the CD.)

Apply to the following sound modifications chart.

Application Exercises
Begin with:

1. *A cappella*

Then:

2. Scales with exercises (and eventually songs)
   (*Listen* to the CD.)

Sound Modifications Chart

Forward Sound	Back Sound	Forward Sound	Back Sound
Hold This Placement	*To Forward Sound*	*Hold This Placement*	*To Forward Sound*
1) Le (as in leak)	La (as in lay)	**3)** Loo (as in lube)	Low (as in low)
2) Leh (as in let)	La (as in lap)	**4)** Luh (as in luck)	Lah (as in law)

These are guides for your air stream placement and not phonetic alphabetic symbols, but are designed to direct the sound forward with comfort as in speech. (For additional advanced exercises, *see* **Vowel Application Chart, Pg. 67.**)

Additional Applications

The following applications are techniques and devices designed to help you move your voice into the forward placement:

- *Imagine **shrinking** (i.e., making smaller) the back vowel and bringing it to a forward vowel position in the mouth along with the front vowel.*

- ***Hold the lips** in an 'oo' pucker, which will bring the back vowels forward to the front of the mouth, holding that 'oo' position for all vowels (your lips will look like a fish).*

- ***Drop the 'oo,'** pucker and shape your mouth to the vowel you are singing or speaking.*

- ***Nasal release:** Apply a silent hum while doing the exercises (e. g., releasing air through the nose without making any additional sound), allowing the air stream to pass unresisted through the nasals, helping the mouth to untrap the throat.*

- ***Imitate a high-pitched cartoon character**, which will bring the sound directly into the nose and mouth.*

- ***Speak*** *low notes on pitch while keeping them on the lips, which will bring them forward into the mouth, letting air flow more easily and releasing any air stream resistance or the tendency to fall in the throat on lower notes.*

Advanced Applications

- ***Deduct the L's*** *after about a month of daily repetitions or when you can keep your sound forward well enough without using the 'L's' partial resistance to help your support.*

  Note: *Remember, deducting the L's will make you use more support from the diaphragm, which will be a little more difficult, but will be more in line with the way you use your voice when you sing. Basically, you are just taking off the training wheels, as it were.*

- *After you feel comfortable with the exercises without the 'L's, then **add 'N's and 'M's** to include the nasals with the oral placement (e.g., 'me', 'may', etc.) holding the nasals open as long as possible to allow the air stream release and resonance to keep working through the nasals as well as the mouth. This also paves the way for the resonant sound used in the following exercises.*

- ***Whisper the note*** *to hear the size of the air stream louder than the sound. This will allow you to experience the feel of the air stream by note size. Also, try silent octaves to hear the difference in air streams (the higher the smaller, the lower the larger). You will hear it and feel it. Close your eyes for better focus.*

- *Add modifications to all vowels and sounds. (See* **Vowel Application Chart, Pg. 73.***)*

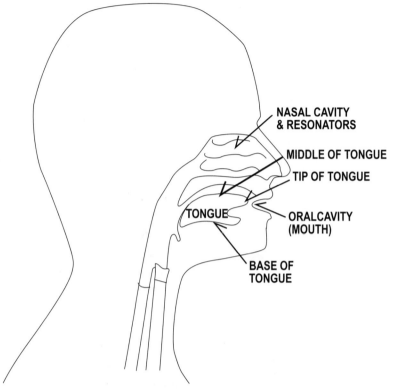

Figure 9: The Oral (Mouth) Cavity
The placement we are concerned with is approximately
from the middle to the tip of the tongue.

Resonance

"Resonance is sound directed into a cavity, which receives and amplifies it into colors according to its structure, determining the quality and volume of that sound. It is the palette of tonality."

Release

"Release is the freedom from air stream resistance in those parts of your instrument that would impede the air flow, therefore allowing the voice its ultimate ability and control."

"Nasal opening adds resonance, in addition to giving the

air stream an additional release."

Exercise #11 ▶ <u>**Nasal Resonance and Release**</u>

Concept

Nasal placement is a **supra-glottal** (i.e., an above-the-vocal-cord) air stream directed to the nasal opening, releasing and resonating the sound. This untraps air in the throat while improving the tonal quality with nasal resonance. *(See* **Fig. 8 and 11** and *listen* to the CD.)

Resonance is simply amplified tonal expansion in a cavity, causing additional coloration (it may be intentional or incidental).

Nasal release, through a silent hum, (i.e., with openness and air only) gives you the feeling of the air flowing through the nose without resonating.

Front nasal resonance is heard through the '**N**', while **back nasal resonance** is heard through the '**M**'. Opening these cavities gives you an awareness of them.

Application

The following exercises are designed to **open up the front and rear nasals**, enabling you to feel and **release the air stream** and initiate **resonance** in the nasal cavity. (*See* **Fig. 11** and *listen* to the CD.)

1) Hum with an 'M'

2) Hum with an 'N'

3) Hum with a 'Mum' (as in mummy)

4) Hum with a 'Nun' (as in none)

5) Hum with a 'Mun' (as in money)

6) Hum with a 'Num' (as in number)

*(The student will demonstrate **two** of the above exercises; **only then** go back and do the remaining four without the student, turning your stereo to the non-student track for scales only to complete the exercises.)*

Additional Applications

- *Literally sing into the nose (like a ventriloquist) and release the pressure in the throat, letting a portion of the air stream rise to the nasals more and more which is where the air stream goes naturally as the notes get higher in pitch. Then go back to a more equal distribution of the sound cavities.*

- *Release air into the mouth and nose simultaneously, creating a fuller, more articulate and brilliant sound, as well as relieving throat compression caused by the upper and lower air stream clashing and creating standing waves. (See **Glossary of Terms**.)*

- *Use the nasals to influence your singing by adding a slight hum to your sound. Balance the sound to your liking.*

Important

➤ **You will get to where you can resonate your nasal cavities with any sound not just 'M's or 'N's. Practice with all sounds.**

"When opened, the throat creates depth of tone in addition to opening and releasing sounds that might normally get stuck in it."

Exercise #12 ▶ <u>Throat Resonance</u>

Concept

You can create **openness, release** and **low-frequency resonance** in your throat without letting notes fall back in it and losing your placement in the mouth or nasals. This is accomplished by keeping the placement forward (*as in* **Exercise 10**) while adding a partial yawn (*as in* **Fig. 10A and 10B**), creating a larger air space in your throat and producing low resonance as well as promoting the release of the air stream in the throat.

The feeling is similar to **yawning** as you're speaking. You're actually still **speaking in your mouth**, although you are opening up your throat by dropping your larynx partially for an instant (creating low resonance) then releasing it back to its normal position at the yawn's conclusion. Extending this condition (i.e., holding the larynx partially down) adds a depth to your sound while you are still using your mouth to speak. This parallels singing by using the mouth to place, articulate and amplify the sound and the throat opening for low-end resonance (like a low-speaking cartoon character).

Application

Use this exercise when you're comfortable holding your placement in the mouth and opening your throat for resonance. If vowels start going back into the throat, stop and return to **Oral Placement (Exercise #10)**, without a yawn.

Use a <u>partial yawn</u> with these exercises:

1) **Resonant yawns**: Sing 'oo' with a partial yawn

2) **Resonant yawns**: Sing 'e' with a partial yawn

3) **Resonant yawns**: Sing 'a' with a partial yawn

4) Sing all vowels, keeping them in the mouth ('a', 'e', 'ah', 'o', 'oo'), using the CD scale with the student side omitted by turning your stereo to one side or the other for self-practice again with a partial yawn.
(*See* **Fig. 5D** and *listen* to the CD.)

Additional Applications

- *Apply the partial yawn to your songs for added depth where desired in various amounts depending on the sound, song or style you desire to create.*

FIGURE 10: THROAT CAVITY

Here the throat is shown open from medium to maximum space. The smaller the space, the less the resonance and release. The larger the space, the more resonance and release. Determine the amount of release and resonance you desire and adjust the larynx somewhere between these two points.

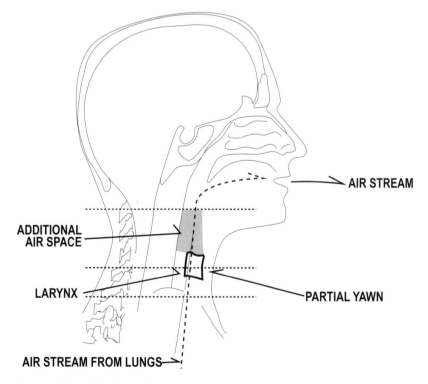

Figure 10A: Medium Openness
The area inside the dark line

The larynx is basically held in a resting position (by external larynx muscles) while singing or exercising.

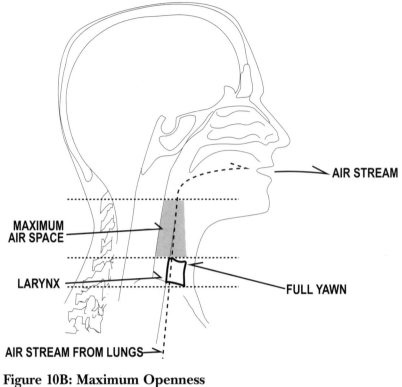

AIR STREAM

MAXIMUM AIR SPACE

LARYNX

FULL YAWN

AIR STREAM FROM LUNGS

Figure 10B: Maximum Openness
The area inside the dark line

The larynx is basically held in a fully dropped position
(by external larynx muscles) creating additional depth while
singing or exercising.

Note: *Using external and not internal muscles to hold the larynx in
place (like a yawn) prevents strain while holding the air passage open.*

All Resonant Cavities

This figure shows the throat, mouth and nasal cavities. Each adds its own contribution to the tonality of your overall sound, as well as an air stream release. The amount of air that is sent proportionally into each cavity will determine the overall release and tonality of the sound, word, phrase, passage, song or style of music. This figure illustrates a visual location for **Exercises 11, 12 and 13.** (*See* **Fig. 11** and *listen* to the CD.) The chest and sinuses add only minimal secondary resonance and are not addressed as a major contribution in this context.

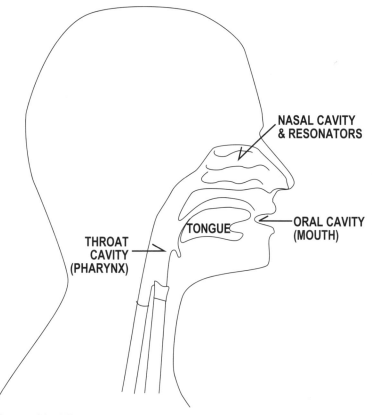

Figure 11: All Resonant Cavities
The above figure shows the locations of the major sound cavities. Use it as a reference for **Exercises 11, 12, and 13**.

"... all the great singers and styles of music rely heavily on resonance and resonators. It can make a marked difference in your sound, depending on how you use it."

Exercise #13 ▶ <u>Oral, Nasal, And Throat Resonance</u>

Concept

Sing a vowel such as an 'oo' forward in the mouth (*as in* **Exercise 10**) and at the same time add a hum in the nose (*as in* **Exercise 9**), then, add a partial yawn in the **mouth** and the **throat** (*as in* **Exercise 3**). Work with combinations of the mouth, nose and throat to increase the resonance in various amounts in each resonator, one after another, then together, while holding the note, to experience the sensation of expansion during singing. I refer to this as **"working the tone."** (*Listen* to the CD.) Listen to and record the difference in the **song performance worksheet (Session Aid #4)**. This will give you the ability to hear many tonal options, including things <u>you</u> want to do stylistically.

You will create different tonal sounds and qualities, adding and releasing resonance in your whole voice. Work toward control in combinations of the above. The more practice, the more control and expansion of the tone, which will give you more facility to improve your tonality. Explore!
(*See* **Fig. 11** and *listen* to the CD.) Remember that all the great singers and styles of music rely heavily on resonance and resonators. It can make a marked difference in your sound, depending on how you use it.

Application

<u>Combinations of Resonance</u>

Do the following:

1) *A cappella*

2) With scales

3) In songs or speech

Using an exercise or music, hold an 'oo' (as in do) in the mouth while opening up one of the following:

1) Nose (partial-hum in the nasals)

2) Mouth (partial-yawn in the mouth only)

3) Throat (partial-yawn in the throat only)

4) 1, 2, 3 (all)
   a) one after another, then
   b) simultaneously

5) Combinations of 1 & 2, 1 & 3, 2 & 3
   a) one after another, then
   b) simultaneously

Note: *Remember to use a lot of support to keep the note going long enough to do 1-5 one at a time or in combinations.*

Concept

This exercise is called the Sob/Whine. The whining is a higher pitched cry directed to a forward placement (much like a puppy whining). The Sob is the low part of a cry (like a deep moan). This stretches the vocal cords by means of the muscles that cause them to expand and contract, as well as enacting a partial yawn. (*Listen* to the CD.)

This tends to hold the vocal cords with more stability as the air stream hits them because of the more active stability (i.e., held in position with the cord muscles) giving the vocal cords more precision, resulting in better pitch, tone and expansion. It also makes it easier to keep the air stream connected above and below the vocal cords without breaks caused by a failing or passive vocal cord or an air stream interruption caused by impedances or mucus on the cord.

This exercise should be done in small amounts at first, building up your ability to use the technique without fatigue. **It's like active muscle building** and must be established slowly to be effective. **Don't overdo it** (begin with a few minutes daily, working up to a little more, as it feels comfortable).

Application

Use:

1) The *a cappella* exercise

Then:

2) The scale exercises

(*Listen* to the CD.)

Note: *Take a rubber band, holding it between the thumb and the index finger and pull gently while observing it stretching and coming closer together. Then pluck it with another finger and listen to the pitch rising like a guitar string. Release slowly and let it contract and observe the looseness between the bands and listen to the pitch go lower. This is very similar to the vocal cord operation and gives you a good illustration due to the audio and visual experience.*

"As the great singers will tell you, a good voice is 'produced,' not used randomly."

| Exercise #15 | Good Vocal Posture |

Concept

A **good vocal posture** is a combination of a portion of the warm-up exercises, setting you up to always have a good **focus, entrance, attack,** and **close** (i.e., always being ready to sing). As the great singers will tell you, a good voice is 'produced,' not used randomly.

The process itself can be called **Vocal Alignment**, always setting yourself up prior to the time that you begin singing or exercising. This **controls the air flow** and **maintains the connection** from the bottom of your lungs right up to your lips (i.e., from your **support, air stream**, **placement** and **resonance** flowing right out into the world) without resistance from your throat and other old habits limiting your ability to sing freely without any impedance. (*See* **Figs. 2B and 2D, 4.1 and 4.2, 5D, 8, 12** and *listen* to the CD.)

Now that you have learned and applied the preceding exercises, putting together groups like this, bring the parts together (i.e., setting yourself up to use your instrument to its optimum at any time and fashion).

"Developing a coordinated independence is using all parts of your vocal instrument together with an individual awareness. This is the process that prepares you to sing from the first note."

INSTRUCTION/APPLICATION

After learning the basic exercises, combining a portion of them together creates Exercise 15, which in reality is a culmination of exercises to create the basics of setting your voice up to sing. This is an important combination of exercises, which enable you to begin a good foundation for other exercises and singing.

1) **Take a deep breath** to expand your chest. Hold it in position (*as in* **Exercise 1, Fig. 2B and 2D**) and **breathe through your stomach** (*as in* **Exercise 2, Fig. 4A and 4B**). As you inhale, open the stomach up quickly—it expands. As you exhale, **firm the stomach,** controlling the air that's going out, causing the stomach to *slowly* move in at the rate you require (*as in* **Exercise 6**) — no longer randomly. **This is the process that controls the air flow of your singing,** releasing air slowly so you can control the speed and volume (amount) of the air stream that you need for proper vocal cord opening and vibration.

2) Maintaining all of the proceeding, **hold a partial-yawn position** (*as in* **Exercise 3, Fig. 5D**) **while singing a front vowel** like 'oo' (*as in* **Exercise 10**) getting the feeling of **your throat being opened up** while **singing forward.** Then keep the throat and mouth open while singing to keep the larynx stable and stop it from jumping up into the breathing passage, as well as adding the desired low resonance in your throat.

3) Next, add a little **'hum'** (*as in* **Exercise 9**) to release air through the nose, unlocking any compression above the vocal cords while adding mid-range tonality and articulation to your sound.

4) Make sure the facial, jaw, and chin muscles are relaxed.

> **Note:** *It may be a little difficult at first to keep all of this in place while singing or doing your exercises, so concentrate on one thing at a time, building up to an overall sense-feel. The more you work with it, the more they will fit together. Eventually, you will develop a sense-memory—which is a memorized feeling for where things are placed. Also, you will develop a coordinated independence, which is using all parts together with an individual awareness. This will prepare you to begin singing from the time you open your mouth (see* **Figs. 2-5 and 9-12**). **Remember three things: practice, practice, practice**. *There is no substitute for a good vocal method practiced regularly. This is the process that prepares you to sing confidently from the first note.*

To monitor the **facial muscles**, lightly place thumbs under the sides of the chin, with forefingers on jaw muscles and let the rest fall lightly on the face. Now, **yawn** while letting the fingers <u>lightly</u> track your facial muscles. Feel the muscles stretch and then return to a relaxed position where they are very soft and pliable. Circles are placed where the fingers and thumb should be (*see* **Fig. 12**).

Note: *This assures you of naturally relaxed head and facial muscles for singing. Do this regularly for all exercises, songs and performances.*

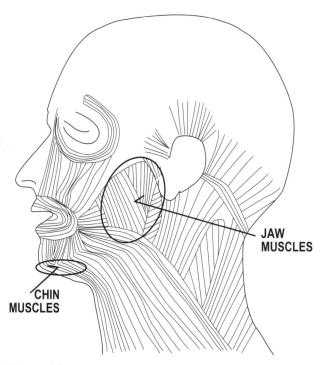

Figure 12: Facial, Jaw and Chin Muscles
This is the key to facial relaxation and monitoring for ease of singing.

"Think about it: Would an athlete go into a performance without first preparing for it? I don't think so! Neither should a singer!"

WARM-UP EXERCISE CONCLUSION

This concludes the *Contemporary Singing Techniques* warm-up segment of the CD (**Segment 1**). Now go back, working with each exercise until it's comfortable enough to proceed to the next one. Don't rush. *"Accuracy and focus are the fundamentals ensuring good basics of singing."*

Additional Applications

- *Use this segment <u>regularly</u> (i.e., 1–2 times daily) to build yourself up for your singing and performances.*

   Note: *Do only a little at first to build up, like running or working out.*

- *You may also want to eventually establish a regular **condensed workout** (i.e., a shortened warm-up) for a daily warm-up prior to singing. Use **Exercises 1, 2, 3, 7, 8, 9, 10, 13 and 15**. Remember to use **Segment 1** to stretch, relax, warm up, and **build up** before singing (just as an athlete does before performing).*

- *Make a cassette of this segment for the condensed workout to use with your tape machines to give you more outlets for practice: home, car, anywhere (duplication is for personal usage only; any other duplication is prohibited by federal law).*

- *If occasionally there is very little time, at least do all your trills, including trilling the songs you are performing.*

<u>Important</u>

➤ **Remember that this CD is set up with the instructor and piano on one side and the student on the other. This way you can eliminate one side or the other if you wish to use it as 1) an accompaniment to emphasize more help, or 2) for a solo performance of an exercise for further development.**

"Working with Bob, I sing with more power, control and ease than I ever have before."

Bob with Meredith Riekse, Alto with The San Francisco Symphony Chorus

"I was shining! The band was amazed...all of the band was so surprised to hear me singing so well."

Vera, Singer with Aikakone
(No.1 Platinum Pop Band, Finland)

"Thank you for putting me in touch with my voice."

Mary Stuart Masterson, Actress

"Bob's voice reminds me of Lou Rawls."

Ted Ashford, Performer/Hit Composer/Songwriter

"He has helped me put what I'm putting down."

Bob with Michael Bloomfield

"You've not only opened a new door through which I can explore more, you've helped me in my everyday delivery."
—Kimberly James

(Left to right) Bama Brown, Bob, Kimberly James, Radio Personality (KVET Radio, Austin, TX)

"You unlock the door to untapped potential."

Bob with Will Thomas, (NBC Anchor)

"Thanks for your skill and your help."

Kitchen Table Wisdom

My Grandfather's Blessings

Dr. Rachel Naomi Remen, Best-Selling Author, Lecturer
(*Kitchen Table Wisdom, My Grandfather's Blessings*)

"...in recognizing of the many outstanding contributions by the local music community..."

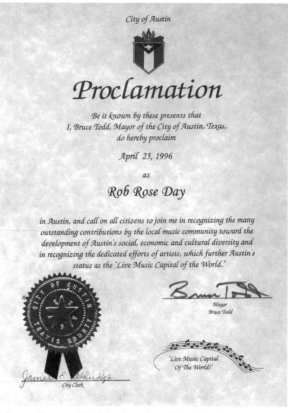

Mayor Bruce Todd, Austin, TX 1996

"Thanks a lot for the vocal coaching."

Tony Ozborne, Lead Singer (Blue Train, Top Ten *Billboard* Single)

*"I would not have
been able to do
this without the
methodology of
Bob Rose."*

William Tracy, EMI International Recording Artist/Producer
(Finland)

*"...in a few short
months, Bob has
shown me how to
overcome my long-
standing vocal
problems."*

Adrienne Harrell, Comedian and Singer

CHAPTER 4

Singing Performance Sessions

(CD Segment 2)

"In our lives, we shall make the most of whatever talents we possess without either sighing for the impossible or fleeing from the inevitable."

—Emmett Fox

Concept

The Singing Performance Sessions of the CD are live, critiqued troubleshooting sessions. They contain live interaction between the instructor and the singer with music tracks similar to Karaoke. This makes it easy for the instructor to stop and start the music and address the singer's problems and begin again, acknowledging their corrections, then beginning their next critiques. This process will be repeated enough times for you to understand what we are accomplishing in a first-hand/second-hand fashion (if you will).

Between the CD and the text, you should pretty much be able to participate and also take the experience of the concept with you for your own material. Go to the sessions introduction for a step-by-step guide to the CD and 1) listen to the sessions; then, 2) participate in the sessions and 3) using the lyric sheet and other "session aids" in this text for the CD song as well as your own repertoire (i.e., applying the same principles and observing the improvements).

"Bob's student evaluation reports rate consistently high for both instructor and course curriculum."
—Mary Son, Program Administrator

Learning Tree University—Los Angeles, CA

An actual troubleshooting singing class where the students came up and sang to a Karaoke-type sing-a-long PA system using sound tracks with a live performance. They were critiqued and re-sang their immediate improvements.

"What an instrument produces depends not only on the state of the instrument, but also upon the musician." —Gary Zukav

SINGING PERFORMANCE SESSIONS

Introduction

To begin, let's take an overview of the sessions before starting. We will address four classic topics in three sessions, as well as the singer's problems: male or female.

I. **Breath Support Session**
II. **Placement Session**
III. **Release and Resonance Session**

In Each Session:

- **First,** the singer will sing a portion of a song all the way through without comments so we can observe any problems. This is called **the preliminary vocal** (CD only).

- **Next**, the singer will sing the song three more times, once for each topic (I, II, and III), and the instructor will stop and **identify the problems, addressing the specific solutions** each time for each topic they are working with. They will **then restart** with the improvement, and sing until a new problem needs attention. This process will be repeated to a successful conclusion for I, II and III above. (*See* the following text and *listen* to the CD.)

  Note: *During this time, the problems and solutions will be defined for the singer and for your understanding as well. Many times there is not just one, but a multitude of symptoms, problems, and solutions in each area of your singing and exercising that must be addressed to put your voice on track.*

- **Then, a corrected performance** to compare the singer's first vocal effort and problems with the application of the new approach. (CD only)

- **Finally, a music track** of the song is provided for you to apply what you've learned and use for your specific problems and solutions. You may want to record this track on your own tape for individual practice. *(Federal law prohibits any other duplication.)*

Important

➤ *We found it better to address one topic at a time for the sake of focus. Remember, you can't do everything at once. You must be comfortable with each solution, one at a time. Then combine more in stages until all corrections are comfortable and become a part of your approach.*

"Breath is the cord that ties the soul to the flesh."

—Paramahansa Yogananda

I. BREATH SUPPORT SESSION

Singer: Problem #1

A breath support problem from not retaining enough air.

Symptoms

The singer is troubled by one or more of the following symptoms:

1) **Shortness of breath**

2) **Going flat** or sharp

3) **Discomfort** in the throat and chest

4) **Fading out** at phrase endings

Problems

1) **Not storing enough air**

2) **Letting air out too fast** by not using diaphragmatic control
   a) **Vocal cords being pulled apart** then over-tightened to compensate for an erratic or over- powering air stream, which creates an unstable larynx and pitch (flat and sharp)

3) **Displacement of the larynx** due to too much air passing through the vocal cords (i.e., forcing the larynx up) and depleting the air in the chest

4) **Using too much air** or not firming the diaphragm enough through the whole phrase

Solutions

Support and control the air stream by:

1) **Holding the chest expanded** and controlling air with the diaphragm (*see* **Exercise 1 and 2**)

2) **Breathing from the diaphragm** and not letting the air be depleted by drawing it from the upper chest and throat instead, using diaphragmatic and abdominal interaction for control (*see* **Exercise 2, Fig. 3** and the **Abdominal Muscles Reference**)

3) **Stabilizing the larynx** with a partial yawn, keeping it from jumping up and blocking the air passage, which causes a feeling of compression and irritation (i.e., tightness and mucus) in the throat and chest (*see* **Exercise 3, Fig. 5D**)

4) **Controlling the air stream** by firming the diaphragm and abdominal muscles and their interaction to control and slow down the air-flow (*see* **Exercise 6 and Fig. 4.1**)

Corrective Performance

The application of these solutions are heard in the singer's performance and will bring about your best performance:

1) **The singer is using an expanded chest and steady support** to maintain and control the air supply (*see* **Exercises 1, 2, 6 and Figs. 2B, 2D and 3**)

2) **The singer is matching the cord opening** with the correct air stream
   (a) stabilizing the larynx with a partial yawn and (*see* **Fig. 5D**)
   (b) firming the diaphragm and abdominal muscles (*see* **Fig. 4.1, and 4.2 and Abdominal Muscles Reference.**)

3) **The singer is using a partial yawn** to drop the larynx (*see* **Fig. 5D**) and **glottal attacks** (i.e., small blasts of air from the vocal cords) to direct the air stream to the oral or nasal cavities or both like a forward grunt. (*Listen* to the CD and refer to the **Glossary** term: glottal attack.)

4) **The singer is controlling the air stream** with the diaphragm and the abdominal muscles in addition to closing notes (i.e., finishing or stopping words. S*ee* **Glossary** term: closing).

"Where your focus goes, your instrument will follow."

Singer: Problem #2

Placement problems: from not bringing sounds forward enough to the mouth or nasals. This section deals with the singer letting the notes fall back in the throat (even if slightly) and trying to force them out instead of placing them forward in the mouth and nasals where they belong.

Symptoms

The singer is troubled by one or more of the following symptoms:

1) **The feeling of forced air** in the throat on certain vowel sounds

2) **Trapped air** in the throat on high notes

3) **Off-pitch** or pitchy sounding

4) **Low notes** falling off; unable to close (i.e., finish or stop) some words

Problems

1) **Vowels resisting or trapping** the air stream caused by the singer **forcing rather than placing** the note where it belongs (i.e., in the mouth and nasals)

2) **Larynx rising**, blocking the air passage (*see* **Fig. 5B**) instead of letting the high-note air stream flow to the mouth and nasals (*see* **Fig. 13**)

3) **Trapped air in the throat** causes pressure on the vocal cords, pulling them apart and causing the singer to go flat. In attempts to hold the pitch, the singer may over-tighten the cords and go sharp as well, trying to compensate for the flatness

4) **Low notes** and/or back vowels falling in the throat interrupting the air stream and the singer is unable to end (or close) the sound or word in the mouth due to it being stuck in the throat

Solutions

Eliminating pressure and any resistance or impedances from the throat (*see* **Exercises 10, 11** and **Fig. 13**).

1) **Vowel air stream modifications:** using forward vowels to lead back vowels forward bringing a consistent flow to the air stream eliminating forcing

2) **Use a forward voice,** singing like a little cartoon character (i.e., small and forward). This is exaggerated for the sake of directing the high notes. When you get used to it, replace the sound with your own voice while staying forward out of the throat

3) **Oral/Nasal releases** a) opening up air passages with a hum (*see* **Exercise 9** and **Fig. 8**), or b) singing in the nose as a temporary over-compensation until the air is released into the nasals naturally, in addition to using c) the mouth by opening it up with a <u>slight</u> yawn (*see* **Fig. 5D**), d) occasionally use a sob/whine to stabilize the note (*see* **Exercise 14**)

4) **Speech articulation,** shrinking the vowels and bringing them forward by <u>speaking</u> them on pitch and ending them as close to the front of the mouth as possible (*see* **Fig. 1B**)

Corrective Performance

The application of these solutions are heard in the singer's performance and will bring about your best performance:

1) **The singer is directing air** to oral and nasal cavities, adding glottal attacks (i.e., percussive blasts) when necessary to eliminate forcing

2) **The singer is letting high notes move up** toward nasals and the front of the mouth as an air release influenced by the use of a forward voice

3) **The singer is placing back vowels forward** into the mouth and nasals (the mixture, depending on pitch, tone and style) untrapping vowels while adding resonance

4) **The singer may speak the melody on pitch,** which will aid in bringing the lower notes to the mouth and nasals, releasing them from the throat

Additional Application

- *Remember to keep your tongue flat and behind the lower front teeth. This will take pressure off the cords and help restore pitch.*

Placement

Vowel Air Stream Modifications

Concept

Vowel air stream modifications are designed to give you an unobstructed airflow, correcting the vowels (single sounds) and diphthongs (double sounds) **by moving their placement** forward, <u>improving pitch</u>, <u>direction</u>, and <u>release</u> of pressure in your throat. This is accomplished by slowing down and adjusting the air stream to properly vibrate the vocal cords (without pressuring them) in context to the size of the cord opening.

Note: *Envision a stream of water controlled by a faucet. The more you open it up the more volume of water and as you close it the less. Imagine it going through a hose without interruption. The stream is broader until you place your thumb over it, gradually causing the stream to become smaller with more pressure and larger when you release it. Each increment of the thumb changes the stream (i.e., more thumb, a smaller stream; less thumb, a larger stream). The diaphragm is like the faucet controlling the air stream to the vocal cords. The vocal cords, like the thumb, and when closer together, vibrate with less air and slightly more pressure; when farther apart, more air results with less pressure which causes the stream to move more freely.*

Instruction/Application

The following is based on the International Phonetics Scale (IPS), (i.e., the normal placement of vowels).

Group I. **Vowels** (single sounds) are arranged so that column **A is the pure sound** and column **B is the "modification,"** creating a forward placement of that sound group, the result of a changed air stream. (*See* **Exercise 10** and *listen* to the CD.)

Group II**. Common Diphthongs** (double vowel sounds) are arranged so that the sound in column **C** is the breakdown of the pure sound (the normal pronunciation) followed by column **D**, which is **the first sound modified and held out**, with the last vowel finishing the sound. The corrected diphthong concludes with the back vowel forward and the forward vowel closing, bringing both together as one sound, not two sounds in two placements fighting each other as diphthongs generally do. (*See* **Vowel Application Chart** and *listen* to the CD.)

Vowel Application Chart

First, go through the columns (A to B then C to D) and say the sounds. **Then** observe them in the appropriate words on the lyric sheets, (male or female) and the "Shorthand Chart Application" to the lyric sheets as well. (*Listen* to the CD **Segment 2**, Placement.)

Note: *This causes you to sing forward while holding the first sound forward and closing with the second sound, which is already forward, bringing them both together at once making them easy to sing.*

GROUP I SINGLE SOUNDS		GROUP II	DOUBLE SOUNDS
Vowels	Modifications	Common Diphthongs	Modifications
A	B	C	D
1) o (go)	oo (new)	1) ah/e......................=I	uh ..../e=I (try)
2) ah (father)	uh (brother)		
3) uh (love)	oo (book)	2) ah/oo.................=ow	Uh...../oo =ou (now)
4) a (at)	eh (pet)		
5) eh (let)	i (it)	3) o/e ....=ouî\ooe	oo ..../e =ooe (boy)
6) i (it)	e (me)		

"Release is the freedom of the air stream to carry the sound without impedance throughout the vocal instrument."

III. RELEASE AND RESONANCE SESSION

Singer: Problem #3

A **release and resonance problem** from not directing the air stream to its optimum destination. This deals with the singer experiencing air resistance and the lack of tonal fullness caused by air stream impedances (mostly above the vocal cords), but occasionally clashing with the air stream below the vocal cords as well.

Symptoms

The singer is troubled by one or more of the following symptoms:

1) The **feeling of thinness** in the voice

2) The **low-end resonance** feels weak with little volume

3) The **high notes are uncomfortable**, feeling trapped and pressured in the throat with little tonality

The Problems

1) The **larynx is being forced** into the breathing passage of the upper throat (almost to a choking position, *see* **Fig. 5B**) instead of staying in its relaxed position (*as in* **Fig. 5A**). It decreases or at times cuts off the opening of the breathing passage in the throat cavity and impedes the air stream eliminating space for resonance and release

2) **Not keeping low vowels placed** forward into the mouth and nasals, dropping them into the throat, which is for resonance not the fundamental note. Also, the diaphragm may be a little lax, causing air to escape to quickly

3) **Not opening nasals and mouth** enough or at all for release and resonance of the high notes

"Resonance is the singer's palate of tonality."

APPLICATION

Solutions

Release: to let the air stream flow freely. Resonance: vibrating the sound in a specific cavity such as the nose, throat, mouth or occasionally the sinuses and the chest.

1) Drop the jaw and open the mouth as much as possible for what you are singing. Maintain the tongue behind the lower front teeth and as flat as possible for each sound, to keep from pulling the larynx up with the back of the tongue, due to its attachment to the larynx (*see* **Fig. 1A**)

   a) **Throat**: Use a partial to a half-yawn for dropping the larynx to activate low-end resonance while opening the throat to untrap the air stream (*see* **Fig. 5D**)

2) **Bring the sound forward:** speak the low note on pitch (i.e., very forward, *see* **Exercise 10**). Using more support (*see* **Exercise 6**), compensating for low notes

3) **Use more oral and nasal release and cavity resonance** producing high-end release and a mid-range resonant articulation of sound. (*See* **Exercises 10 and 11**.)

Corrective Performance

The application of these solutions are heard in the singer's performance and will bring about your best performance:

1) **The singer opens the throat** for more space, release, and resonance without dropping the vowel into the throat

2) **The singer is now directing the low sound** toward the mouth as in speaking (using glottal attacks, if needed) with more support for the larger rate of air moving for low notes

3) **Now the singer is opening the mouth and nasals** for release and resonance of high notes, using the 'M' and 'N' feeling with an open mouth for a more forward sound. This aids in untrapping the high-note air stream

"Sound waves naturally gravitate to their own size cavity...."

FIGURE 13: WAVE SIZE CHART

Concept

Sound waves naturally gravitate to their own size cavity according to acoustic principles. Consciously follow their lead and send your sound in that direction: lows to the mouth, highs to the nasals. Do not force the pitch up or down, but help direct it to the placement it wants to travel toward, be it the mouth or the nasals or both but not the throat. Keeping the air directed to the mouth and nasals will help it flow with release and resonance without getting stuck in the throat. After a while, you'll develop a sense-feel and a sense-memory for the correct (i.e., the easiest) placement. The following figures will show you a wave (heading toward its cavity) as an example to give you an image to envision the sound produced without resistance, therefore letting the notes go where they naturally want to.

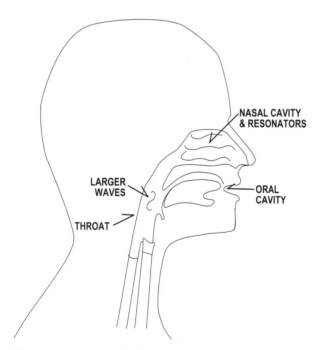

Figure 13A: Large Waves
As lower frequencies (i.e., pitches) fall, the air stream and the notes travel lower toward the mouth as the stream arc bends and becomes rounder (as water from a hose when it is turned down).

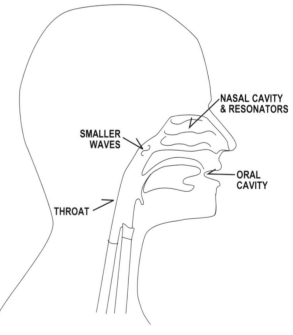

Figure 13B: Small Waves
As higher frequencies (i.e., pitches) rise, the air stream and the notes travel higher toward the nasals in addition to the mouth as the stream arc becomes straighter (as water from a hose when it is turned up).

CHAPTER 5

Session Aids

Concept

The following aids are designed to help you visualize the verbal corrections in the CD song sessions (**Segment 2**), as well as to provide a reference and application of the session's method for your own songs.

Go over each aid and its interaction with the others until they become clear; then work with them until they become second nature.

This will greatly enhance your understanding of this method and make it easier to apply to your own material and style.

SESSION AID #1

Performance Shorthand Chart

Singing Chart Symbols
(For Songs)

Example: The following symbols are a basic shorthand method for correcting general singing problems. They are used in conjunction with the lyric sheet (to follow) as a road map for immediate solutions to eliminate common hidden technical problems. Slang symbols are used instead of proper phonetics for the sake of ease and simplicity of use. **These symbols are placed above a word as a reminder of the action required.**
(*See* **Lyric Sheet** altered example, then apply on the unaltered lyric sheet for your vocal.)

NO.	SYMBOL	ACTION	PURPOSE
1	S	Support: breath control (sustained (short/long) firming of the stomach muscle, which in turn will firm the diaphragm muscle, as in **Exercise 6**) need to use it at	Controlling air flow at your own desired speed through the interaction of the stomach and diaphragm muscles which holds back the air to the speed you
2	/	Breathe here	Indicates where to take a breath in preparation for the following phrase line or word
3	O	Open up: symbol used over any sound to indicate opening the mouth/nose/throat	For the release and resonance of a sound through or in a cavity
4	M	Open the mouth (generally keeping the tongue down and behind the lower front teeth)	For more release, resonance, volume and larynx stability
5	N	Open the nasals (back, front or both). For back nasal sound use an 'M' <u>feel</u> (not M). For front nasal sound use an 'N' <u>feel</u> (not N) (*See* **Exercise 9**)	For release and resonance of a sound in the nose as well as mid-range articulation in your overall sound
6	T	Open the throat by dropping the larynx slightly without dropping the note back in the throat by using a partial to a half-yawn (**Fig. 5D**)	For a release and resonance of a sound in the throat creating more depth in your sound
7	∧	This symbol indicates to bring the sound forward (vowel air stream modification)	To release the air stream from the throat, directing it to the mouth and/or nasals
8	Y	Drop the larynx with a partial yawn (*see* **Fig. 5D**)	To increase release and low resonance in the throat
9	›	Glottal attack (a plosive): a percussive blast of air like a grunt directed forward (*see* **Glossary of Terms**)	To direct the air stream or to put an edge on a sound
10	C	Close, complete or stop the word with proper enunciation and concluding good support.	For good, sharp word and air stream endings. For good pitch
11	P	Control plosives such as B, D, K, P, S, etc., by slightly separating the enunciators	Eliminating the popping or 's' ing sounds, etc.

Figure 14: Performance Shorthand Chart

<u>Lyric Sheet (Altered Example)</u>

Male

Follow along with the music on the CD and observe the changes over the words (based on **Fig. 14, Performance Shorthand Chart**) then, apply to the unaltered lyric sheets for your vocal. (*Listen* to the **Singing Session** on the CD.)

"Brand New Day"
Music & Lyrics by Steve O'Neill
©1999 Steve O'Neill

<u>Verse</u>

WHAT IS THE REASON YOU TURN OUT THE LIGHTS

CAN YOU NO LONGER STAND THE PAIN

OR IS THE REASON YOU'VE JUST HAD ENOUGH

LIVING IN THE SHADOW OF SHAME

AND IN THE MORNING DO YOU REALLY SEE THE TRUTH

OR DO YOU SIMPLY TURN AWAY

AND IN THE EVENING WHEN YOU TURN OUT THE LIGHTS

DO YOU BELIEVE IN A BRAND NEW DAY

<u>Chorus</u>

BRAND NEW DAY

BRAND NEW DAY

WE ALL NEED A

BRAND NEW DAY

Lyric Sheet (Altered Example)

Female

Follow along with the music on the CD and observe the changes over the words (based on **Fig. 14, Performance Shorthand Chart**) then, apply to the following unaltered lyric sheets for your vocal. (*Listen* to the **Singing Session** on the CD.)

"Five Lonely Days and Lonely Nights"
Music & Lyrics by Bob Rose,
Lee Parvin, & Dessda Zuckerman
©1986 Easy Feat Music, Inc.

Verse

```
                ^
                oo                    s
THE VERY FIRST PHONE I SEE IN MEMPHIS
     ^                        ^
     uh                       oo
I'LL CALL YOU UP TO LET YOU KNOW
   ^         ^      ^       ^
   uh      uh/e     e       uh
I GOT MY MIND MADE UP ON LOVIN' YOU
                         ^
                         uh              ^     ^
                                         eh    oo   C
FROM THE MINUTE MY HEART WALKS BACK THROUGH THAT DOOR

(CAUSE IT'S BEEN)
```

Chorus

```
     ^         ^
     oo        e              ^
                              uh    C
FIVE LONELY DAYS AND LONELY NIGHTS
                                        ^          ^
                                        oo         uh/e
SINCE WE HELD EACH OTHER LOVING THROUGH THE MORNING LIGHT
   ^                                         ^
   uh                    O                   uh/e
TOUCHED EVERY FEELING DREAMED WITH EVERY SIGHT
     ^         ^        ^          ^         ^
     uh/      oo        e          oo        uh/e
IT'S BEEN FIVE LONELY DAYS AND LONELY NIGHTS
```

Song Performance Worksheet

Stop to address one problem at a time in the parts of the song in which it occurs (like the sessions on the CD). Rectify each one and note it on this worksheet along with a warm-up exercise that may help in the solutions. Then, proceed to **Fig. 14**, using the following unaltered lyric sheet for your own road map, as the previous ones, only for your own performance.

Worksheet
List of Problems and Solutions

Problems:	Solutions (Including Exercises 1-15):

Make additional copies of this page for yourself to use with your own songs. (All other copying without permission prohibited by law.)

Figure 15: Song Performance Worksheet

<u>**Lyric Sheet**</u>
(Unaltered)

Male Song

Use this unmarked lyric sheet to make your own road map, using the **Performance Shorthand Chart, Fig. 14,** for your own solutions. **Use the altered chart** made for the singer on the CD as an example for your own vocal.

"Brand New Day"
Music & Lyrics by Steve O'Neill
©1999 Steve O'Neill

<u>**Verse**</u>

WHAT IS THE REASON YOU TURN OUT THE LIGHTS

CAN YOU NO LONGER STAND THE PAIN

OR IS THE REASON YOU'VE JUST HAD ENOUGH

LIVING IN THE SHADOW OF SHAME

AND IN THE MORNING DO YOU REALLY SEE THE TRUTH

OR DO YOU SIMPLY TURN AWAY

AND IN THE EVENING WHEN YOU TURN OUT THE LIGHTS

DO YOU BELIEVE IN A BRAND NEW DAY

<u>**Chorus**</u>
BRAND NEW DAY

BRAND NEW DAY

WE ALL NEED A

BRAND NEW DAY

<u>Lyric Sheet</u>
(Unaltered)

Female Song

Use this unmarked lyric sheet to make your own road map, using the **Performance Shorthand Chart, Fig. 14**, for your own solutions. **Use the altered chart** made for the singer on the CD as an example for your own vocal

"Five Lonely Days and Lonely Nights"
Music & Lyrics by Bob Rose,
Lee Parvin, & Dessda Zuckerman
©1986 Easy Feat Music, Inc.

<u>Verse</u>

THE VERY FIRST PHONE I SEE IN MEMPHIS

I'LL CALL YOU UP TO LET YOU KNOW

I GOT MY MIND MADE UP ON LOVIN' YOU

FROM THE MINUTE MY HEART WALKS BACK THROUGH THAT DOOR

(CAUSE IT'S BEEN)

<u>Chorus</u>

FIVE LONELY DAYS AND LONELY NIGHTS

SINCE WE HELD EACH OTHER LOVIN' THROUGH THE MORNING LIGHT

TOUCHED EVERY FEELIN' DREAMED WITH EVERY SIGHT

IT'S BEEN FIVE LONELY DAYS AND LONELY NIGHTS

Self-Troubleshooting Worksheet

Use this worksheet for each song to remember its parameters as well as a reference and cross- reference to common occurrences between songs. This will help eliminate problems quicker as they will become clearer and more focused (once you've noted and compared song to song). *

User Page

Singer: Song:

The **singer** explains <u>the **symptoms**</u>:	The **singer** notes <u>the **problems**</u>:
1)	1)
2)	2)
3)	3)
4)	4)
5)	5)
Additional Notes/Comments:	Additional Notes/Comments:
<u>**Solutions**</u>: (Notes as you experience them) 1)	<u>**Corrective Performance:**</u> (Notes on <u>your</u> solutions) 1)
2)	2)
3)	3)
4)	4)
5)	5)
Additional Notes/Comments:	Additional Notes/Comments:

*Make additional copies of this page for yourself to use with your own songs. (All other copying without permission prohibited by law.)

Figure 16: Self-Troubleshooting Worksheet

Common Vocal Range Charts (Female and Male)

These ranges are common to most applications. Your voice may vary, spilling into other ranges, higher or lower or both. These charts provide a basic reference only.

Figure 17A: Female Vocal Range

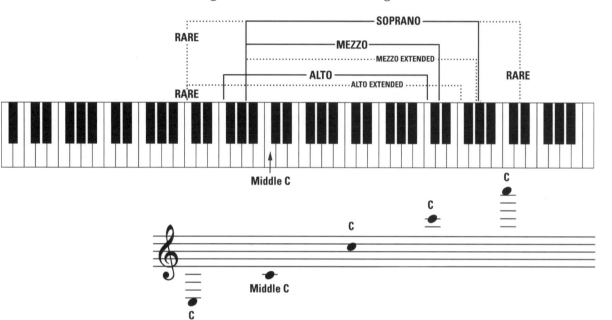

Figure 17B: Male Vocal Range

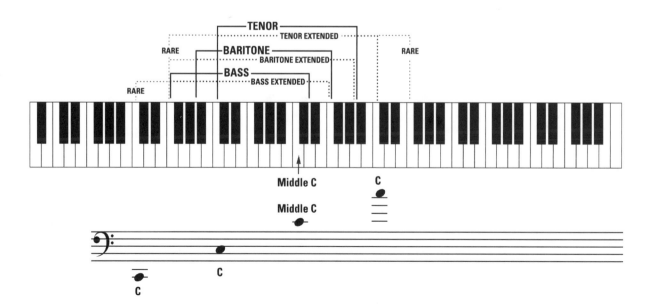

Glossary of Terms

The definitions listed are only those that may be in question or come up often in this book. This is not meant to be a dictionary nor a complete text glossary. For further definitions, see the *Harvard Dictionary of Music*, a good audio dictionary and an abridged *Webster's Dictionary*, if desired.

- *A cappella*: without music (i.e., voice(s) only)

- **Aural:** as heard by the ear

- **Breath Mark (/):** a slash indicating to take a breath at that sign

- **Close/Closing:** ending words by stopping the air stream (aural or silently) to conclude a sound with a consonant via the diaphragm, glottis or articulators

- **Compression:** opposing pressures such as a sub-glottal air stream (below the vocal cords) pushing up with a trapped supra-glottal air stream (above the vocal cords) not releasing, creating an impedance or a stoppage in airflow. This limits the movement of the larynx; trapping, pushing up or impeding it from doing its job

- **Entrance:** the approach into a word, phrase or song

- **Epiglottis:** a fleshy flap located at the top of the larynx, below the back of the tongue, used to prevent solids or liquids from going down into the trachea (breathing tube) and ultimately the lungs. It is what reacts when something is *going down the wrong way*. This has nothing to do directly with the sound except choking or coughing and blocking the wrong elements from going down the trachea

- **Exit:** the finish of a word, phrase, section, or song

- **Forward:** bringing the sound more toward the front of the mouth and/or nasals via a free flowing continuous air stream

- **Glottal Attack:** a plosive pulsation of air initiated from the vocal cords and usually brought to the mouth or nose or combinations of both. It gives direction to sound, helps pitch, opens and closes notes and can add an edge quality (if desired) to a sound as well. (*Listen* to the CD.)

- **Larynx:** the "*voice box*" in your throat, which contains the vocal cords, false cords, the glottis and their muscles, as well as many other parts not mentioned in this text

- **Mouth Placement:** directing the airflow and sound to the oral cavity (mouth)

- **Nasals:** the nose and its components

- **Nasal Placement:** directing the airflow and sound to the nasal cavities (nose)

- **Opening Up:** generally opening the resonant cavities (the mouth, nose, throat or combinations) for the release and resonance of the sound

- **Pharynx:** the throat (*see* **Figure 1A**)

- **Placement:** where the sound goes

- **Plosive:** a blast of air generated by the diaphragm, vocal cords, articulators, or soft palate

- **Oral:** the mouth

- **Release:** to unimpede or let flow

- **Resonance:** to open and vibrate air cavities, including the mouth, nose and throat, (secondarily the sinuses and chest) for extended tone and/or volume

- **Sense-Feel:** feeling the sound's vibration in a certain place

- **Sense-Memory:** subconsciously retaining the sense feel

- **Soft Palate:** the soft flesh on the roof of the mouth beginning where the hard palate ends and concluding where the uvula begins

- **Standing Waves:** notes pushing each other from two different directions, causing a collision and jamming sound into a specific place

- **Sub-glottal:** the air stream coming from under the vocal cords

- **Sub-texting:** as in a movie script, interpreting the meaning, intent and motive of the words by lines, sections, or song, etc., noted in a single word or thought in the margin of the lyric sheet for reference

- **Support:** to activate, control and regulate the air supply below the vocal cords, (a sub-glottal air stream) initiated by means of the stomach and diaphragm muscles working in coordination and interaction with one another (*see* **Exercises 1, 2 and 6**)

- **Supra-glottal:** the air stream above the vocal cords

- **Sympathetic Vibration:** a resonator vibrating in sympathy to a note triggering a pitch off in its cavity

- **Uvula:** the soft U-shaped tip of flesh hanging from the end of the soft palate over the top of the throat, which directs the air stream and the sound to the mouth and/or nose

- **Vowel Air Stream Modifications** (also referred to as "Vowel Modifications"): a method discovered by the author, using a technique of unimpeded airflow to enable a controlled air stream (above and below the vocal cords) without being resisted by the vocal instrument's components (based on the International Phonetics Alphabet (**IPA**)

- **Yawn:** used as a device to **1)** relax the throat and **2)** lower the larynx. Yawns release, amplify and resonate the throat, mouth and occasionally the nose—**a)** a full yawn is used for relaxation **b)** a partial to a half-yawn is used for opening the throat as a release and creating more space in that cavity for resonance

Conclusion

"Clarity evaporates fear." —Gary Zukav

This concludes the *Contemporary Singing Techniques* CD and reference text. Keep working with the CD and the text until a complete understanding is achieved. Then use the warm-up segment daily and begin applying the technique to your own material. Use this text as a **supplement** and **reference** at any time for additional clarity.

Reference Texts

The Voice as an Instrument
by Ramon Rizzo

The Voice and Voice Therapy
by Daniel R. Boon

The Anatomy Coloring Book
By Kapit and Elson

The Vowel
by Russell McGrath

The Larynx
by Marvin P. Fried

Gray's Anatomy
by John A. Crocco, M.D.

Harvard Dictionary of Music
by Apel and Daniel

The Seat of the Soul
by Gary Zukav

Caruso's Method of Voice Production
by P. Mario Marafioti

Modern Recording Techniques
by Robert Runstein

Illustrated Flute Method
by Stokes and Condon

The Studio Handbook
by John Woram

About the Author

Bob Rose is a Vocal Trainer/Coach as well as an active vocalist. He has worked with such artists as The Beach Boys, Mary Stuart Masterson (actress), Michael Bloomfield, singers from the San Francisco Symphony Chorus, *Sister Act* (the Movie) and many others. He instructed classes, seminars, and workshops for The Dick Grove School of Music (L.A.), Sherwood Oaks College for Recording Arts (Hollywood), Learning Tree University (L.A.), Master Vocal Classes for NARAS' Grammy in the Schools at the University of Texas (Austin, Texas). In 1996, he received the Music Achievement Award from the Mayor of Austin, Texas. He has written articles, columns and has been written up in well-known music publications for several years, as well as authoring vocal texts including *Contemporary Singing Techniques, The Ins and Outs of Breathing*, and *Vocal Hygiene*. He currently instructs voice at his own studio in San Francisco where he lives with his family, as well as performing and recording as a vocalist.